I want to be a Zookeeper

I WANT TO BE A

Zookeeper

DAN LIEBMAN

FIREFLY BOOKS

A FIREFLY BOOK

Published by Firefly Books Ltd. 2003

First Printing 2003

Publisher Cataloging-in-Publication Data (U.S.)
(Library of Congress Standards)

Liebman, Dan.
   I want to be a zookeeper / Dan Liebman.—1st ed.
[24] p. : col. photos. ; cm. – (I want to be)
Summary: Photographs and easy-to-read text describe the job of a zookeeper.
ISBN 1-55297-699-8
ISBN 1-55297-697-1 (pbk.)
1. Zookeepers – Vocational guidance 2. Occupations.
I. Title. II. Series
331.124163 21   HD8039.Z66.L54   2003

Published in the United States in 2003 by
Firefly Books (U.S.) Inc.
P.O. Box 1338, Ellicott Station
Buffalo, New York, USA., 14205

National Library of Canada Cataloguing in Publication Data

Liebman, Daniel
   I want to be a zookeeper / Dan Liebman

ISBN 1-55297-699-8 (bound)
ISBN 1-55297-697-1 (pbk.)

1. Zookeepers – Juvenile literature. I. Title

QL50.5.L53 2003   j636.088'9'023   C2002-903690-9

Published in Canada in 2003 by
Firefly Books Ltd.
3680 Victoria Park Avenue
Toronto, Ontario, Canada, M2H 3K1

Photo Credits

© Ken Ardill, page 13
© Thomas Curro/Henry Doorly Zoo, pages 10-11
© Nubar Dakessian/Toronto Zoo, pages 16, 24
© Jeff Greenberg/Firstlight.ca, page 15
© Dick Haneda/Toronto Zoo, pages 22-23
© Julie Hanna/Toronto Zoo, page 17, front cover
© Stephen Homer/Firstlight.ca, pages 5, 6-7
© Maraya Raduha/Toronto Zoo, page 18
© Nick Rensink/Toronto Zoo, back cover
© R. Watts/Firstlight.ca, page 19
© George Walker/Firefly Books, pages 8, 9, 12, 14, 20, 21

The author and publisher would like to thank:

The Toronto Zoo for its assistance and expertise, including the following individuals:
Maraya Raduha, Jennifer Martin, Janis Miller,
Gavin Small, Juliana So, Shelley Stewart, John Stoner,
Ted Strikwerda, Cathy Wilding, Shanna Young

Design by Interrobang Graphic Design Inc.
Printed and bound in Canada by Friesens, Altona, Manitoba

The Publisher acknowledges the financial support of the Government of Canada through the Book Publishing Industry Development Program for its publishing activities.

Zookeepers do many different jobs. They keep animals happy and healthy.

Zookeepers make sure that the animals and their homes are clean. This elephant is getting a bath.

Zookeepers look after all kinds of animals. This zookeeper knows a lot about snakes.

How tall is a giraffe? Does it sleep standing up? Zookeepers answer many questions.

Penguins are from a very cold place, but they feel at home in the snow.

The animals in the zoo are from all over the world. This hornbill comes from India.

The zookeeper gives this baby special attention.

The kangaroos are learning to trust this zookeeper.

Dolphins are very smart. They understand what the zookeeper is saying.

This zookeeper tells the tree kangaroo that she is a very good mother.

The koala is going to be weighed. Zookeepers make sure animals eat enough.

This fruit bat likes to follow the zookeeper all day long.

Zookeepers don't usually get this close to wild cats. This cheetah was raised by hand and trusts the keeper.

These large stick insects are also part of the zoo family.

It's time for the camel to be brushed. Zookeepers make friends with all kinds of animals.

The zookeeper and the baby rhinoceros are getting to know each other.

A zookeeper's day is a busy one. There's so much to do! Playing with the animals can be the best part of the job.